Primix Publishing
485c US Highway 1 South
Suite 100
Iselin, NJ 08830
www.primixpublishing.com
Phone: 1-800-538-5788

Published by Primix Publishing: 09/12/2024

ISBN: 979-8-89194-245-5(sc)
ISBN: 979-8-89194-246-2(e)

Library of Congress Control Number: 2024913592

Any people depicted in stock imagery provided by iStock are models, and such images are being used for illustrative purposes only.

Certain stock imagery © iStock.

Because of the dynamic nature of the Internet, any web addresses or links contained in this book may have changed since publication and may no longer be valid. The views expressed in this work are solely those of the author and do not necessarily reflect the views of the publisher, and the publisher hereby disclaims any responsibility for them.

Consonants "v, x"
辅音字母 "v, x"

1. Draw a line to the picture that makes the same sound as "v".
   将发 "v" 音的图片连线。

2. Draw a line to the picture that makes the same sound as "x".
   将发 "x" 音的图片连线。

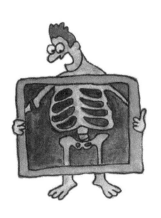

5

Consonants "th, cl"
辅音字母组合 "th, cl"

1. Draw a line to the picture that makes the same sound as "th".

   将发 "th" 音的图片连线。

2. Draw a line to the picture that makes the same sound as "cl".

   将发 "cl" 音的图片连线。

Compound Words 复合词

Draw lines between the words to match the picture on the left. 将两个单词连线并与左边的图片相配。

○ bee   slid

○ cup   hive

○ rain   fall

○ snow   coat

○ sail   boat

○ ear   ring

Mixed-up Sentences
顺序混乱的句子

Example

The words in a sentence should be in order.

The bridge, the, over, is, water.

The bridge is over the water.

The words for each sentence are out of order. Write each sentence with words in order.
下列每个句子的单词顺序不对，请按顺序连成一句。

1. swimming, is, A fish _____

_____

_____

_____

2. are, trees, two, There _____

_____

_____

_____

Maze ; Finding alphabet A to Z

Look at the picture below. Help Kenny find alphabet A to Z and also find number 1 to 10 in this picture. All the letters and numbers are hidden under the rocks and trees.

找字母 A 到 Z

看图，帮助男孩找到字母 A 到 Z，数字一到十并画圈。

Selecting word ending "d"
选择以 "d" 结尾的单词

Take a look at each picture in the box. Circle the same ending sound of the picture above. 看方格里的每一幅图片，将与上面图片相同尾音的图片画圈。

cold

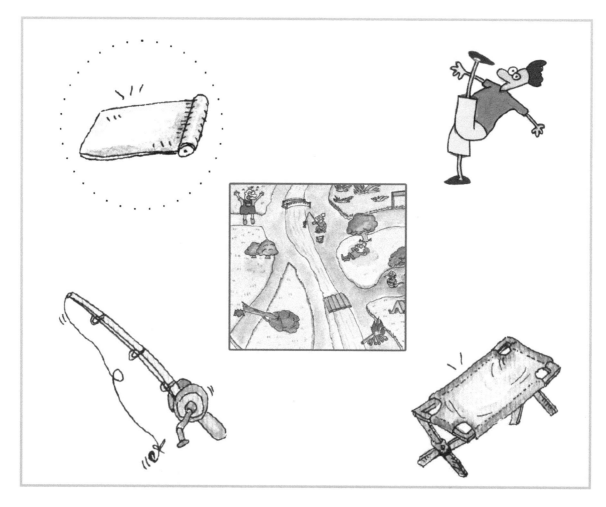

Rhymes: ending "d"

Matching word with the picture
搭配单词与图片

Name each picture on the left. Read each word on the right. Fill in the circle next to the word with the picture. 给左边的每一幅图片命名，读右边的每一个单词，将正确的图片单词前的圆圈涂满。

1.
○ mud
○ braid
○ mad

2.
○ shed
○ cod
○ rod

3.
○ sad
○ head
○ bird

4.
○ mad
○ toad
○ cot

5.
○ sad
○ bed
○ bird

6.
○ sad
○ head
○ toad

Rhymes: ending "d"

Word recognition-ending "d"

单词辨认 – 以 "d" 结尾的

Name each picture below. Find the ending sound and the letter of each picture. Print the rest of the letters in the blank.

给下面的每幅图命名，找到每幅图的尾音和字母，将其剩余的字母填到空白处。

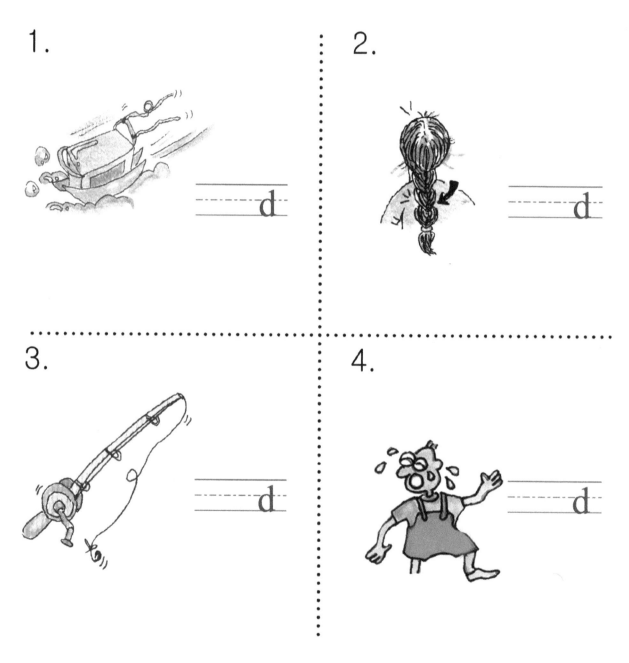

1. _____ d

2. _____ d

3. _____ d

4. _____ d

Rhymes: ending "d"

Making a sentence 造句

✿ Use all the words you learned from the picture above the line.
Make a complete sentence below the line. 用你在横线上的图片中
所学到的单词，在横线下造一个完整的句子。

| sled | sad | bird |

The boy is ＿＿＿＿＿.

Two boys are riding on the ＿＿＿＿＿ .

Rhymes: ending "d"

Selecting word ending "p"
选择以 "P" 结尾的单词

✽ Take a look at each picture in the box. Circle the same ending sound of the picture above. 看方格里的每一幅图片，将与上面图片相同尾音的图片画圈。

sip

Rhymes: ending "p"

Matching word with the picture
搭配单词与图片

Name each picture on the left. Read each word on the right. Fill in the circle next to the word with the picture. 给左边的每一幅图片命名，读右边的每一个单词，将正确的图片单词前的圆圈涂满。

1.
- ○ sharp
- ○ talk
- ○ peep

2.
- ○ pig
- ○ top
- ○ pop

3.
- ○ soap
- ○ log
- ○ cube

4.
- ○ hog
- ○ leap
- ○ harp

5.
- ○ bed
- ○ ship
- ○ bird

6.
- ○ sad
- ○ head
- ○ deep

Rhymes: ending "p"

16

❀ Name each picture below. Find the ending sound and the letter of each picture. Print the rest of the letters in the blank.
给下面的每幅图命名，找到每幅图的尾音和字母，将其剩余的字母填到空白处。

1.

_____ p

2.

_____ p

3.

_____ p

4.

_____ p

Rhymes: ending "p"

17

Making a sentence 造句

chimp   peep   harp

A boy is peeping that ------- is playing

the -------.

Rhymes: ending "p"

18

Selecting word ending "n"
选择以"n"结尾的单词

Take a look at each picture in the box. Circle the same ending sound of the picture above. 看方格里的每一幅图片，将与上面图片相同尾音的图片画圈。

yarn

Rhymes: ending "n"

Matching word with picture
搭配单词与图片

1.
○ horn
○ phone
○ pan

2.
○ bean
○ apple
○ wagon

3.
○ pen
○ pan
○ tan

4.
○ raccoon
○ clay
○ pen

5.
○ man
○ bed
○ bird

6.
○ sad
○ hen
○ toad

Rhymes: ending "n"

Word recognition-ending "n"
单词辨认－以"n"结尾的

✿ Name each picture below. Find the ending sound and the letter of each picture. Print the rest of the letters in the blank.

给下面的每幅图命名，找到每幅图的尾音和字母，将其剩余的字母填到空白处。

1.

_____ n

2.

_____ n

3.

_____ n

4.

_____ n

Rhymes: ending"n"

Making a sentence 造句

Use all the words you learned from the picture above the line.
Make a complete sentence below the line. 用你在横线上的图片中
所学到的单词，在横线下造一个完整的句子。

raccoon   horn   wagon

A   raccoon   blows the _____

on the _____.

Rhymes: ending "n"

22

You can find fun stories below the picture. You can also describe whatever you like.

* I am now in "Dumbo" island.
* Wind surfing
* You are on the wrong way here.
* Secluded village home
* Public opera house
* Add 5, otherwise you won't pass here.
* Have you tasted a truely delicious soup ?
* It is made of a shocking shark spin ?

23

You can find fun stories below the picture. You can also describe what ever you like.

Let's have a fun!

* My skill is popping out of the water.
* Skidding down   * Isn't this right?
* I'll teach you how to pass.
* ③You come this way!
* I am a cross country swimmer.
* Have you heard a giant yellow tail ball fish?

Adding up all the numbers together make the total numbers come out 50.
There are nothing but two ways to meet our friends.
While we keep on sailing canoe, we'll meet the friend "#16" eventually.

Let's have a fun!

24

Special Noun and Pronoun
特殊的名词和代词

✿ Naming words include places, persons, animals or things. Look at the word box and fill the word in the blank next to the picture.
给下列单词命名，包括地点，人，动物和事情。看词盒里的单词，在图片旁边的空白处填空。

kid	school	lock	ox

Place

_____

Person

_____

Thing

_____

Animal

_____

✿ See the pictures and write the words under the line.
看图片在横线下写单词。

A _____ is riding on the _____ .

25

Making a sentence 造句

cow

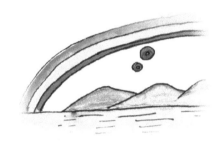

rainbow

window

The _____ can see a _____ after

raining.

Words that describe 描述词

See the picture on the right and describe the scene as much as possible. Fill in the blank with the action verb in the box.
看右边的图，并尽可能多的描述场景。 指出词盒中的行为动词填空。

- She is _____ a turkey.

- The boy is wating to _____.

- The man is _____.

- The market _____ various kinds of vegitables.

- The man who wears suit is _____ a paper bag on the top of his head.

crying, pay, holding
carrying, displays

Naming part / action part

名词 / 动词

Match each naming part with an action part to make a sentence. 将左边的名词和右边的动作词语连线，并连成一句。

Naming Part	**Action Part**
1. The woman	is shouting to the woman.
2. The rain	is chopping the meat.
3. The man	is sliding down.
4. The butcher	is falling down.
5. She	is ordering meat.

Making a sentence 造句

Look at the picture and words above the line. Fill in the blank and make a proper sentence below the line.
看横线上面的图片和单词，在横线下的空白处写下正确的句子。

A boy   strings   ballons

A boy is ———————   ————————— .

Look at the picture and words above the line. Fill in the blank and make a proper sentence below line. 看横线上面的图片和单词，在横线下的空白处写下正确的句子。

Jane   leash   a   dog   walks.

She ————   **a** ————.

It's ranch 农场

❊ Some children here do what most of kids do in the city. Circle things that does not usually happen in the ranch. 农场的孩子们和大部分城市的孩子们做的事情一样。将下面不属于农场的事情画圈。

❊ Choose the pictures you have found and then trace and write the words down in the space. 选择你已经找到的图片将单词写到空白处。

g _____   t _____   v _____   h _____

31

Look at the picture below and make your own stories. Compare yours with ours.

Please find me and point to the scene in this picture. I turn into a general holding swords and guns among these little rascals; kicking the ball, targeting the face of the pirate, running over and screwing up somebody's picnic, throwing the ball to the hitter and all the stuff is messed up... ext.

在图中，
你喜欢什么活动？
用英语描述！

This Little Light of Mine

This lit-tle light of mine, I'm gon-na let it shine.

This lit-tle light of mine, I'm gon-na let it shine.

This lit-tle light of mine,   I'm gon-na let it shine, let it

shine, let it shine, let it shine.

2. I feel it when I'm happy,
   I'm gonna let it shine.
   I feel it when I'm sad,
   I'm gonna let it shine,
   I feel it when I'm lonely,
   I'm gonna let it shine.
   Let it shine, Let it shine,
   Let it shine.

Consonants "wh, cr"
辅音字母组合 "wh, cr"

1. Draw a line to the picture that makes the same sound as "wh".

   将发"wh"音的图片连线。

2. Draw a line to the picture that makes the same sound as "cr".
   将发"cr"音的图片连线。

Finding words from the picture
从图片中找单词

See the picture and find the words from the word box. Write down the words in the blank. 看图从词盒里找出单词，并写到空白处。

1. How many buildings can you see in the picture?

2. Circle the car which is between blue and yellow car.

3. What is the girl doing?

4. What color is the bus?

5. Is the girl walking?

Word Box

wave   blue   red

brown   walking   siting

Thinking patterns with the picture
用图片造句

IV. Circle the picture that goes together with the first picture in each row. 将每一行中与第一幅图片可以连成一句的图片画圈。

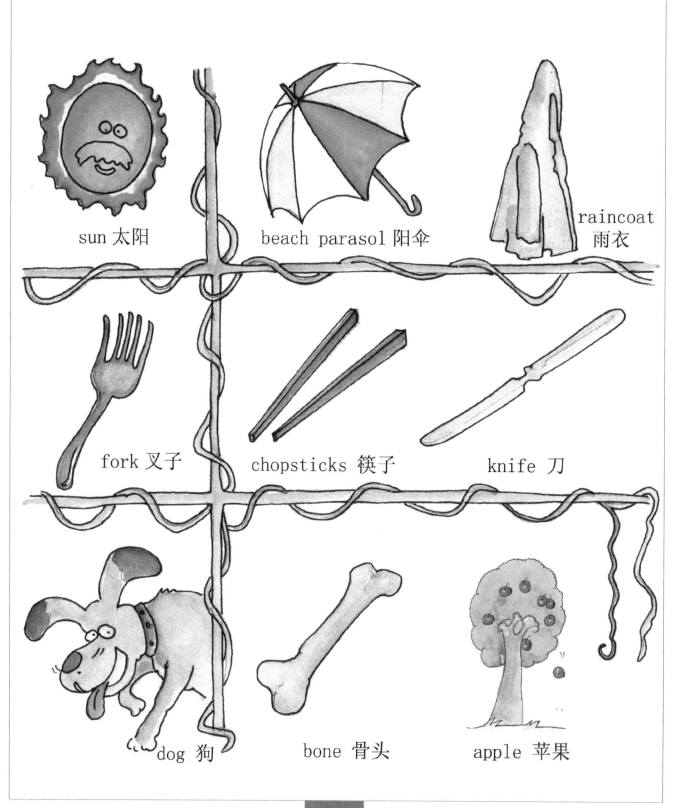

sun 太阳   beach parasol 阳伞   raincoat 雨衣

fork 叉子   chopsticks 筷子   knife 刀

dog 狗   bone 骨头   apple 苹果

Selecting words from the picture
从图片里选单词

Word box

teacher, poem, hand,
point, student

教书先生 t___ch___

古诗 p___m

学生 s__u_e___

站着 st__n__

手 h__n__

指 p___nt

Finding words from the picture
从图片中找出单词

Look at the picture and say its name. Circle all the picture that has the same ending sound. Select words which hide from clouds, mushrooms, and the number 6 from the picture.

看图并说出它的名称，将含有相同尾音发音的图片画圈。将躲藏在云彩，蘑菇，数字 6 旁边的单词挑选出来。

stand

站立
____

读
____

头疼
____

Joy

快乐
____

跳舞
____

Read

dance

headache

Matching words to the picture
搭配单词与图片

○ lung
○ long
○ song

○ talking
○ fighting
○ sleeping

○ pushing
○ paying
○ point

○ going
○ drying
○ painting

Words with picture 图片单词

Pick the words from the cloud box. Write it down in the blank next to the picture.

在云彩中挑出单词，在图片旁边的空白处写下来。

gem box   jewelry   bird

鸟 _____

盒子 _____

珠宝 _____

Choosing words from the picture
从图片里选择单词

See each picture below and find the proper word next to it.
Circle the word that names each picture and print the word.

看下列每一幅图片，找出其旁边正确的单词，将每幅图片的正确单词画圈，
并写出这个单词。

jeep
jewelry

珠宝

strange
strong

奇怪

dream
driver

梦

see
sea

看

heel
help

帮助

box
fox

盒子

Easy words with picture
简易的单词与图片

Write the correct word that stands for each picture from the word box. 从词盒里找出代表每一幅图片的正确单词写下来。

word box

Jewerly, argument, crying, bird

1. Women like _____ very much.

珠宝

2. The _____ has wings to fly.

鸟

3. Peter and Tom have an _____ about the subject.

打赌

4. The baby is _____.

哭

43

✿ Some people do not belong to this scenary. Find and circle things or people that could not be seen in this ranch. 有一些人不属于这个场景，请将在农场里看不到的人或事物画圈。

✿ Choose the pictures you have found and then trace and write the words down in the space. 选择你已经找到的图片将单词写到空白处。

C

Z   W   S

Addition and subtraction

加法和减法

Follow the arrows to count numbers. 跟随箭头数一数。

1. How many sharks can you watch?

   If a fisherman catches 2 sharks, how many sharks are left?

2. How many fishes can you count in all?

3. The man who is swimming wants to take 5 fishes out of water.

   How many fishes will be left ?

Naming Words 给单词命名

✿ Look at the picture and fill out the words and then circle the right words. 看图，找出单词并且将正确的单词画圈。

1. I do like to _____ the food.

           eat

           buy

2. Do you want to go to _____ of the mountain?

           the top

           river

3. I don't _____ good.

           feel

           tell

4. I'd like to _____ the books on the shelve.

           sell

           read

Word game puzzle

字谜游戏

Can you help me solve the crossword puzzzle?
你能帮我解这个字谜游戏吗？

Cross

1. We call cat this way sometimes. _____

2. People enjoy riding _____ .

Down

3. The animal has two horns. _____

4. Sleep is rhyming with _____.

| kitten | horse | sheep | goat |

Naming part / action part
名词 / 动词

Match each naming part with an action part to make a sentence. 将左边的名词和右边的动作词语连线，并连成一句。

Naming Part	Action Part
1. The sign	is making a face.
2. The boy	is standing
3. He	says"Keep off flowers!".
4. He	is streching his arms.
5. He	tiptoes across the garden.

48

Mixed-up Sentences
顺序混乱的句子

Example

The words in a sentence should be in order.

The picture, the, on, hangs, wall.

The picture hangs on the wall.

The words for each sentence are out of order. Write each sentence with words in order. 下列每个句子的单词顺序不对，请按顺序连成一句。

1. The pet, the bed, sits, on.

_____

_____

2. shining, The moon, is.

_____

_____

Action verb / Describing pictures
动词 / 描述图片

See the picture above and describe the scene as much as possible.
Fill in the blank with the word in the box.
看上面的图片尽可能多的描述场景，用下面所给的行为动词填空。

- A man is _____ the purse to the begger.

- A dog is _____ up at the man.

- The begger is _____ at the purse.

- The bearded man _____ up.

- The kid _____ riding the skateboard.

thumbs	donating	stops	surprised	looking
冲击	捐赠	停止	惊奇	注视

50

Nouns and Pronouns 名词和代词

♣ See the pictures and sentenses, circle two nouns in each sentence. 看图片和句子，将每个句子中的两个名词画圈。

I)

    1. The girl reads a book.

    2. She listens to the songs from the
       music box.

II)

    1. The boy plays the hockey.

    2. The driver waves his hand angrily.

 From the picture above, find some special nouns. Then write special nouns in the blank. 从上面的图片中找出每一个特殊名词，将其写在空白处。

1. The girl, Amie sings a song.   _____

2. The boy, Jack wears hockey gloves.   _____

Missing letters 遗漏的字母

♣ See the words in the box that go along with the pictures below.
Fill out the missing letter in the space.
看词盒里的单词，在空白处填写遗漏的字母。

s__cc__r   b__at   c__r   f___its

♣ Draw lines to the pictures that match each other.
将人们要去的地点图片画线。

One and more than one
一个或多于一个的

❀ See the picture of the market, and then check out whether the word on the picture is "singular or plural". Circle the right answer and write the word in the blank. 看这个市场的图片，检查一下图片上的单词 是单数还是复数。将正确的答案画圈并抄写每一个单词。

1. watermelon
   watermelons

2. banana
   bananas

3. egg
   eggs

4. bottle
   bottles

5. turkey
   turkeys

53

Action Word 动词

The action words are the verbs that show action.Take a look at the picture and put the action verb in the blank from the word box. 动词是表示动作的单词。看图将词盒里的单词写到空白处。

---- Word Box ----

reads, holds, shouts, carries, raises, rings
读， 抓住， 大喊， 拿， 举起， 铃响

1. The monk (   ) his bell.

2. Police (   ) his bat up to the sky.

3. Joe (   ) the news paper.

4. Jessie (   ) a giant carrot.

5. Jannie (   ) up her one leg.

6. He (   ) hurray to his winning team.

Sentence 句子

✿ Look at the picture and circle the right sentence.
看图片，将正确的句子画圈。

1. A boy flies high with the swing.
   a boy flies high with the swing.

2. A boy with a red shirt puts a sausage
   into his uncle Joe's mouth.
   a boy with red shirt puts a sausage
   into his uncle Joe's mouth.

3. a man's hat flies off from his head.
   A man's hat flies off from his head.

✿ See the picture above and write the correct words that begins with each the sentence. Write the correct ending mark. 看上面的图片，写出正确的单词开始每个句子。 并在结尾写上正确的标点符号。

1. | Who | .... is eating the sausage ....
   | What |

2. | When | .... does the boy play ....
   | Where |

55

Past tense "ed" and special form of verb
动词的过去式 "ed" 形式和特殊形式

1. We went to the movie.

_____

_____

2. She talked to the man.

_____

_____

3. He paid the money.

_____

_____

4. He painted the tree.

_____

_____

Using "is" or "are"　"is" 或 "are"

See the picture, and fill in the blank using "is" or "are".
看图，并 "is" 和 "are" 填空。

1. There (　　　　) a ship sailing on the sea.

2. There (　　　　) two animals and one umbrella shown in the

   picture.

3. The man and the woman (　　　　) talking each other.

4. The seal (　　　　) spinning the ball on the nose.

5. The chick (　　　　) holding the umbrella.

6. The man in the window (　　　　) showing his finger and talking

   to somebody.

Compound Word 复合词

See the picture in each row. Fill in the line with a correct word to the picture. Make a complete compound word to the line. 看每一行的图片，将图片的正确单词写到横线上组成一个完整的复合词。

58

Finding words 找单词

See the box words and the arrows. Move the number of spaces on the arrows. Write the letters to make the complete words.
看下列盒子里的单词并跟随箭头，在开始处开始每一个单词，
按箭头指向移动数字代表的位置，并将该位置的字母写下来构成新的单词。

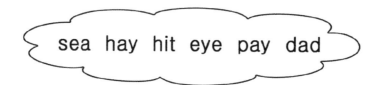

sea hay hit eye pay dad

Start

| e |
| d |
| i |
| t |
| m |
| h |
| p |
| y |
| s |
| a |

 ↓10 ↑9 ↓9 = **sea**

↓6	↓4	↑2	= _____
↓6	↑3	↓1	= _____
↓7	↑3	↑2	= _____
↓1	↓7	↑7	= _____
↓2	↓8	↑8	= _____

59

Word meaning 单词的含义

Choose the word from the word box, and fill the word in the blank. 用词盒里选出的单词，并填到空白处。

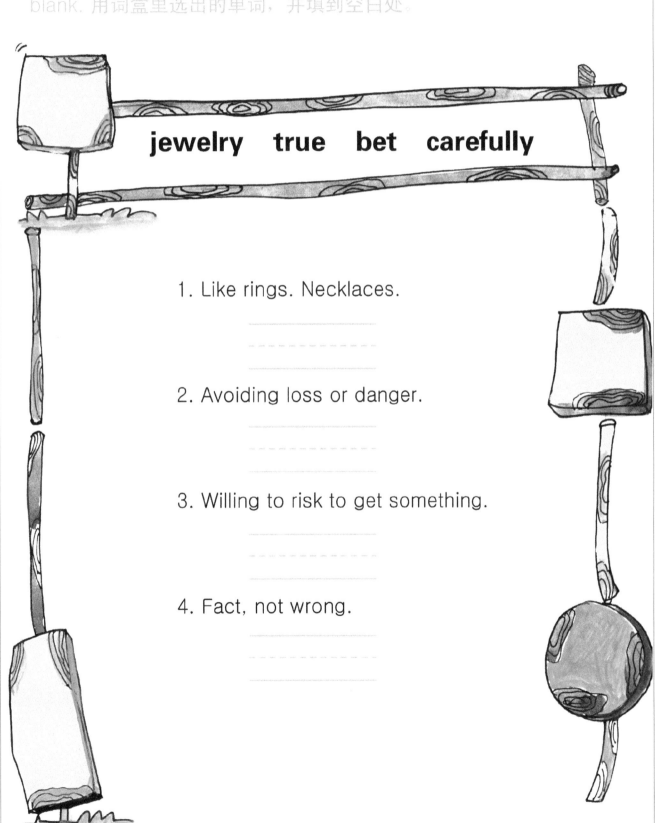

jewelry   true   bet   carefully

1. Like rings. Necklaces.

2. Avoiding loss or danger.

3. Willing to risk to get something.

4. Fact, not wrong.

3

61

"There Were Ten in the Bed."

1. There were ten in the bed and the lit-tle one

said, "Roll o- ver, roll o – ver." So they

all rolled o- ver and one fell out.

2. There were nine in the bed...
(verses 3–9–count one less each repetition)

10. There was one in the bed and the
little one said, "I found it!"

Questions/Sentences 问题 / 句子

✽ Read the sentences below. Find the correct sentence and underline it.
读下列的句子，并找出正确的句子，在底下划线。

I)

1. She cradles her baby.

   She cradles her baby?

2. Is she smiling to the baby?

   she is smiling to the baby.

3. There are a pillow in the bed.

   Is there a pillow in the bed?

II)

1. The girl is fat.

   Is the girl is fat?

2. The angel play a harp.

   Does she look angry?

3. she is angry.

   Is she angry?

✽ When the letter begins wtih the sentence, the first letter is capital. Circle the correct letter and write it on the blank. 当一个单词位于句首的时候首 字母要大写，将正确的字母画圈并写下来。

| she / She | _____ opens the music box _____ | ? / . |
| The / the | _____ kid sits on the roof _____ | . / ? |

Problem solving 解题

Follow the arrows to count numbers. 根据箭头数数。

1. A boy is holding _____ pink baloons.

_____ yellow baloons.

_____ red baloons.

_____ blue baloons.

How many baloons is he holding in all?

2. Juggler is throwing _____ red

_____ blue balls through the air very quickly.

How many balls he is throwing through the air in all?

3. There are _____ flowers in the flower garden.

Somebody picks away 3 out of them, how many flowers are left?

Problem solving 解题

Use the picture to solve each problem. 根据图片填空。

1. There is _____ milky cow and _____ bull.

   There are _____ sheep.

   How many cow and sheep are there in all?

2. There are _____ sheep.

   There are _____ ducks..

   The farmer take 3 sheep away.

   How many sheep and ducks are left?

3. There is _____ rabbit.

   There are _____ ducks.

   The hunter takes one rabbit and 2 ducks away.

   How many rabbit and ducks are left?

Sentence 句子

看这幅图片，在每一个问题下划线并回答下列问题。

1. Does she eat apple?

2. Does she wear jeans or a skirt?

3. What color does she wear?

看这幅图片，在每一个问题下划线并回答下列问题。

1. What is the boy doing?

2. Does he put on socks?

Cumulative review/Question

66

Sentence 句子

✿ Look at this picture. Draw a line under each question and answer the following questions.
看这幅图片，在每一个问题下划线并回答下列问题。

1. What does he do?

2. Does he stand alone?

3. He stands alone.

✿ Look at this picture. Draw a line under each question and answer the following questions.
看这幅图片，在每一个问题下划线并回答下列问题。

1. What does he play?

2. What color top does he wear ?

3. He is running.

Cumulative review/Question

Addition 加法

1.

$$3 + \boxed{} = 10$$

4   7   9   11
○   ○   ○   ○

2.

$$5 + \boxed{} = 9$$

1   7   4   8
○   ○   ○   ○

3.

$$4 + \boxed{} = 9$$

2   7   5   8
○   ○   ○   ○

4.

$$2 + \boxed{} = 9$$

5   7   9   8
○   ○   ○   ○

$$\begin{array}{r} 7 \\ + \quad 3 \\ \hline \end{array}$$

$$\boxed{}$$

$$\begin{array}{r} 9 \\ + \quad 0 \\ \hline \end{array}$$

$$\boxed{}$$

1. 2 rabbits are playing around the forest, 3 sheep join them. How many animals are there?

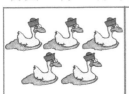

○ 5 + 2 = 7

○ 2 + 4 = 6

○ 5 + 3 = 8

Addition 加法

✤ Find the missing number that makes the number sentence true and fill in the bubble with the right answer. 选择所缺数字使下列格式正确，并将正确答案前的圆圈涂满。

1.

2 + 5 = ☐

| 2 | 7 | 9 | 11 |
| O | O | O | O |

2.

3 + 7 = ☐

| 2 | 7 | 9 | 10 |
| O | O | O | O |

✤ Add the number and use counters if you like. 加数字。

```
   4          3          4          7
+  9       +  3       +  4       +  2
_____     _____     _____     _____
[    ]     [    ]     [    ]     [    ]

   0          0          3          5
+  7       +  8       +  5       +  3
_____     _____     _____     _____
[    ]     [    ]     [    ]     [    ]
```

✤ See the picture below and solve the problem. 看下列图片解题。

1.There are 7 birds and 3 sheep. How many animals are there in all?

2. There are 3 bees and 3 sheep. How many bees and sheep in all?

Sentence 句子

🍀 Look at this picture. Draw a line under each question sentence. And then answer the following questions.

看这幅图片，在每一个问题下划线并回答下列问题。

1. What does the kid play?

2. What does he hold?

3. He is sad.

🍀 Look at this picture. Draw a line under each question and answer the following questions.

看这幅图片，在每一个问题下划线并回答下列问题。

1. Is she brave or scared?

2. Why she is so scared?

Cumulative review/Question

Descriptive 描述

Look at the pictures below. Write the right adjective that describes each picture and write down the words on the line.
看下列图片写出描述每幅图片的正确的形容词并写在横线上。

cute	scared	smile	danger
可爱的	害怕的	微笑	危险

1. It is (　　　　　) for him to play in the middle of the road.

2. The driver is so (　　　　) of the boy jumping into the car.

3. Mom is giving her (　　　) to her baby.

4. The baby is so (　　　).

Descriptive adjective

Word game puzzle 字谜游戏

w				f		n
	s					

Reference Box

spider	car	cool
smart	feet	bird

Adjective 形容词

sleepy	high	tasty	bald	slippery	fatty
困的	高的	美味的	光头的	滑的	肥胖的

_____

_____

_____

_____

_____

_____

_____

Descriptive adjective

Naming part / action part
名词 / 动词

Match each naming part with an action part to make a sentence. 将左边的名词和右边的动作词语连线，并连成一句。

Naming Part	Action Part
1. The boy	is sitting on the chair.
2. Big glasses	is holding a jug.
3. The ship	are laid on the ground.
4. The housekeeper	is sailing.
5. The woman	is holding a paper.

Match each naming part with an action part to make a sentence. 将每一个名词和相应的动词搭配，造句。

Naming Part	Action Part
1. The tall man	holds out his arms.
2. The small man	is smiling.
3. A man	are talking each other.
4. They	is dressed up.
5. A man with hat	point his fingers.

1. Draw a line to the picture that makes the same sound as "sn".
   将与 "sn" 发音相同的图片连线。

2. Draw a line to the picture that makes the same sound as "sp".
   将与 "sp" 发音相同的图片连线。

spin	hockey	crying
snow	sprinter	sneege

People are shopping in the market. Some items are not sold in this store. Circle the items which do not belong to the supermarket. 人们正在商场购物，有一些商品在这家商场没有把不属于这家超市的商品画圈。

Choose the pictures you have found, trace and write the words down in the space. 选择你已经找到的图片将单词写到空白处。

S   c   r

S   s   r

Vowel sound "i" 长元音"i"

Biting is fun.

"kite" has long a "i" sound. Name each picture and circle the picture which has a long "i" sound. Choose the word from the word box and write it in on the line next to the picture.

"kite" 含有长元音"i"。给每幅图片命名，将含有长元音 "i" 的图片画圈。

word box

time,cry,busy,find, fly,smile

时间 _____

笑 _____

飞 _____

哭 _____

找 _____

忙 _____

78

Finding acting verbs 找出行为动词

Name each picture. Circle the correct word for the picture. Find acting verbs from the picture. 每幅图片命名，将代表图片的正确单词画圈，找出图片中的动词。

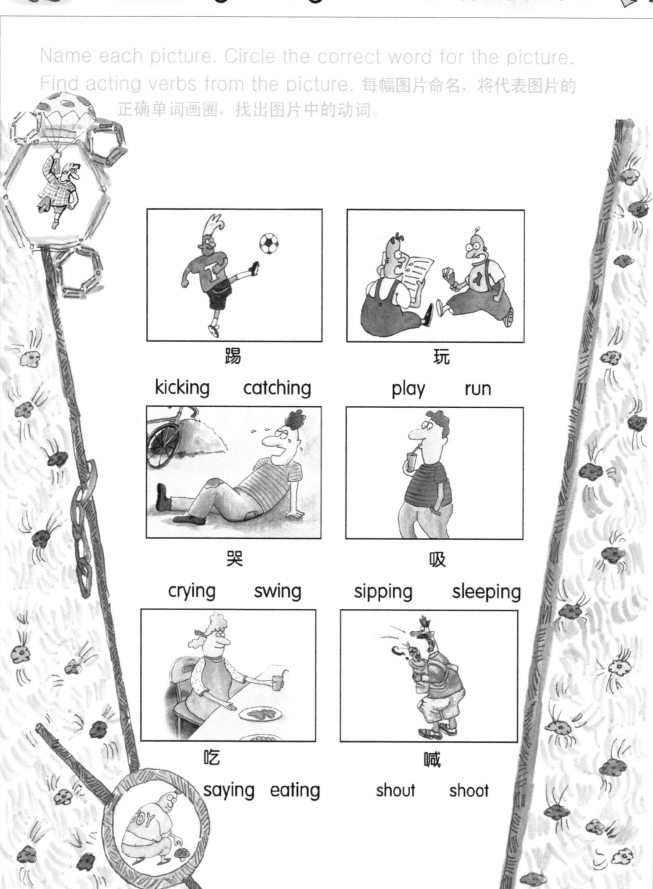

踢

kicking   catching

玩

play   run

哭

crying   swing

吸

sipping   sleeping

吃

saying eating

喊

shout   shoot

79

Descriptive verbs from the picture
描述图片的动词

word box

sweating, running, sleeping, sitting, exercising, delivering.

81

Put your own word for making stories here!

START

I beat it!

Boy, I'm the winner!

*Puke, it's disgusting! *Keep the nature clean!
*I'm sorry, I have to pee on you.
*Holy cow! What a scene!
*It's maginificient! *Iron gate
*Have you heard a huge mountain shark?
*I'm a mountain pirate looking for salmons!
*I barely escaped this before, but what is it now?
*This is another big one!

This is real Adventure you might come across mountains; pirate, shocking shark or even much scaring dizzy cliff, easy to falling off.

Vowel 元音音韵

Read the sentence and see whether the underlined word is spelled right or wrong. Write the correct word on the line if it is wrong.

读句子，看一下化线单词的拼写是否是正确的单词。

Left ○→right, right ●→wrong.

1. There is a big <u>hiv</u> on the tree

   _____

2. It's a <u>sunny</u> day.

   _____

3. The mom bear is <u>shaking</u> a tree.

   _____

4. Three bees are <u>buzing</u> all around.

   _____

5. A baby bear can't wait to eat <u>hony</u>.

   _____

Selecting words with picture
选择正确的图片单词

See the picture and find the word in the word box.
看图并在词盒中找出单词。

1. How many buildings can you see in the picture? (   )

2. Circle the car which is between blue bus and yellow car.

3. What is she doing ?   She is ------------

4. What color is the bus ? ------------------------------

5. Is she walking or sitting?

She is ------------------------

Waving, blue, red, yellow, walking, siting.

Ending consonant review
复习辅音结尾的单词

♣ Take a look at each picture. Choose and circle the right ending consonant to the picture.

看每一幅图片，选择图片名称的正确辅音尾音，并画圈。

(f , p)

(g , r)

(n , k)

(m , n)

(l , r)

Vowel A (ai/ay)

元音 A(ai/ay)

Read the sentence in each row with the picture; circle and write the word in the sentence.

读句子，将符合句意的正确单词画圈，并写在句子中。

○ play
○ grey
○ cry

1. Boys (   ) the table tennis.

2. Train runs the (   ) road.

○ rail
○ tray
○ sail

3. When do you (   ) your boat?

○ pail
○ snail
○ sail

4. He (   ) the bill at the counter.

○ plain
○ pay
○ play

○ trail
○ pail
○ quail

5. A (   ) will fly to the sky.

Long a (ay and ai)
长元音 a (ay and ai)

Say the name of the picture above the line.
说出横线上图片的名称。

tail

train

sail

See the picture above and fill in the blank with the proper words.
看上面的图片并将正确的单词填空。

The dog wags his _____ to the _____ .

5

"THE ANTS GO MARCHING ♪~"

The ants go march – ing one by one. Hurrah!_____ Hur – rah! _____ The
ants go march–ing one by one. Hurrah!_____ Hur – rah! _____ The
ants go march–ing one by one. the
lit–tle one stops to suck his thumb,and they
all go march – ing
down to the ground to get
out of the rain. BOOM! BOOM! BOOM!

2. The ants go marching two by two,
   Hurrah! Hurrah!
   The ants go marching two by two,
   Hurrah! Hurrah!
   The ants go marching two by two,
   the little one stops to tie his shoe,
   and they all go marching
   down to the ground
   to get out of the rain.
   BOOM! BOOM! BOOM!

Soccer game kicks off with our gangs!

看图编故事

All our family members come here! Take a look at the picture. Make a great story on your own!

Soccer game kicks off with our gangs!

看图编故事

All our family members come here! Take a look at the picture. Make a great story on your own!

Horray, Horray, I beat it!
Voicing up a great supporter.
How come you hit my nose?
I'm going to give you a ticket.
My nose is almost broken.
You got a yellow card?
This scene should be recorded by the camera.
One of my son's shoes is taken off to high!
Don't give him a warning card!
It will be ok if the shoe is falling off.
I'm injured so bad, but relaxing myself is not bad at all.
I am lying on the stretcher.

Finding words 找单词

See the box words to follow the arrows. Begin each word at Start. Move the number of spaces on the arrows and write the letters to make words. 看下列盒子里的单词并跟随箭头，在开始处开始每一个单词，按箭头指向移动数字代表的位置，并将该位置的字母写下来构成新的单词。

toy   hot   net   oat   cat   cab

Start

↓2	↓1	↓2	= toy

e
t
o
r
y
n
h
a
b
c

↓10	↑2	↑6	=
↓6	↑5	↓1	=
↓3	↓5	↑6	=
↓10	↑2	↓1	=
↓7	↑4	↑1	=

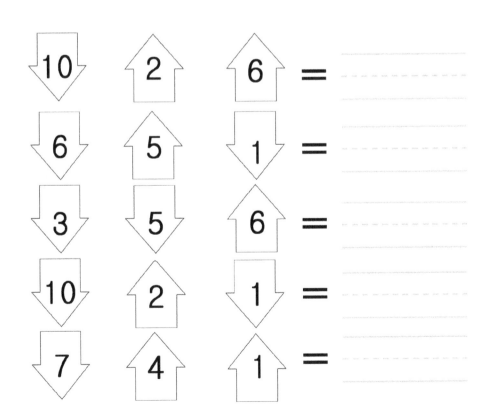

91

Finding words 找单词

See the box words to follow the arrows.Begin each word at Start.
Move the number of spaces on the arrows and write the letters to
make words. 看下列盒子里的单词并跟随箭头，在开始处开始每一个单词，
按箭头指向移动数字代表的位置，并将该位置的字母写下来构成新的单词。

pay day tea say dad sat

Start

☀ ↓9	↑1	↑2	=	**pay**

e
i
t
r
u
y
s
a
p
d

↓10	↑2	↑2	=
↓3	↑2	↓7	=
↓7	↓1	↑2	=
↓10	↑2	↓2	=
↓7	↓1	↑5	=

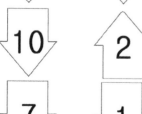

92

See the words box to follow the arrows. Begin each word at start. Move the number of space on the arrows and write the letters to make words. 看下列盒子里的单词并跟随箭头，在开始处开始每一个单词，按箭头指向移动数字代表的位置，并将该位置的字母写下来构成新的单词。

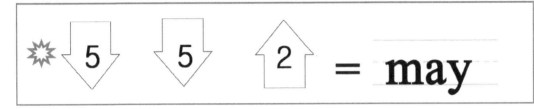

may did key sit pit kit

start

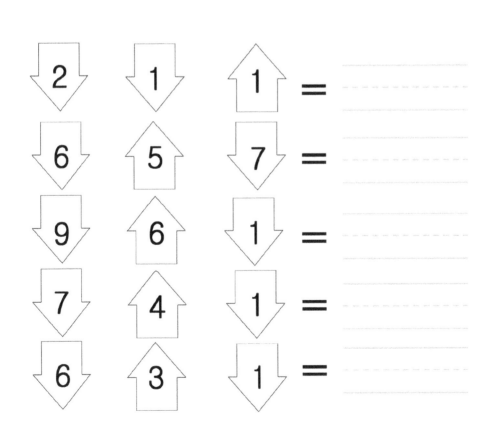

↓5	↓5	↑2	= **may**

↓2	↓1	↑1	=
↓6	↑5	↓7	=
↓9	↑6	↓1	=
↓7	↑4	↓1	=
↓6	↑3	↓1	=

e
d
i
t
m
k
p
y
s
a

Questions and subtraction 减法题

❋ Question1) 问题 1

5 pigs are eating food around the pen. 2 pigs out of 5 set off from the pen after they finished their dinner. How many pigs are still eating now？ 5 只小猪正在猪圈旁边吃东西，有两只小猪在它们吃完以后离开了猪圈。现在还剩几只小猪正在吃东西？

❋ Question 2) 问题 2

There are 6 cats in the living room. My sister took 3 cats out. How many cats are left there? 客厅里有 6 只猫，的妹妹拿走了 3 只，还剩几只？

❋ Question 3) 问题 3

Find the missing number that makes the number sentence true and fill the bubble in the right answer. 找出缺少的数字，使列式正确，将正确答案前的圆圈涂满。

1.

$$8 - \boxed{} = 3$$

5   2   1   4
○   ○   ○   ○

2.

$$9 - \boxed{} = 3$$

3   4   6   7
○   ○   ○   ○

Addition 加法

There are 7 birds in the trees. 2 more birds just flew down to sit on the same branch. How many birds are there in total ?
树上有 7 只鸟，又有 2 只飞过来坐到了同一个树干上，一共有多少只鸟？

✿ Question 2) 问题 2

8 puppies came to Tom's door. There were 2 dogs there sipping the soup. How many dogs are there in total?
8 只小狗来到了汤姆家的门口，在那儿有 2 只狗在喝汤。一共有几只狗？

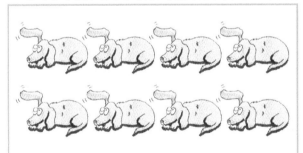

✿ Question 3) 问题 3

Find the missing number that makes the number sentence true and fill the bubble in the right answer. 找出缺少的数字，使列式正确，将正确答案前的圆圈涂满。

1.

$$7 + \boxed{} = 9$$

1   2   3   4
○ ○ ○ ○

2.

$$8 + \boxed{} = 10$$

4   2   9   11
○ ○ ○ ○

❋Question1) 问题 1
Read the sentence. Write the word that matches each meaning from the word box. 用词盒里的单词，完成下列句子。

> eagerly, slowly, loudly, peeping, lonely, seen.

1. You must drive your car _____ when you see the school bus.

2. The doggy inside of the box is _____ out.

❋Question 2) 问题 2
Use the word from the word box above and print it with the same meaning.

1. Feel sad _____ .

2. Very interested in doing something _____ .

✿ Question1) 问题 1

Suffixes are added to the end of a word to change its meaning: "ful, ly". 在词后面加后缀，可以改变词的意思。

1. A dog is _____ a bone _____ .

2. Sometime, she feels _____ .

3. The dog _____ a cat _____ .

4. The man _____ the dog _____ .

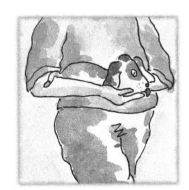

licking, carefully, quickly, carry, eagerly, chased, lonely.

One slightly wet and moist day, the dog, Kenny caught a terrible cold. He was so wet when he splashed into the puddle at the backyard the other day.

It rained heavily all over the place where he usually played well. He sneezed hard and had a fever. So he was brought to the vet. He was taken not once, not even twice, but more than 5 times. He had a spoonful of medicine not once, but he had six spoonfuls of medicine.

Sara, Kenny's owner worried about him. She rolled him back and force to check out his body. She caressed and stroked his back gently and lovingly. She patted his tummy several times saying "poor little puppy".

A dog taken to the vet 小狗去看兽医

1) How much medicine did Kenny take? 它吃了多少药？

2) Why did he go to the vet? 它为什么要去看兽医？

3) Was it sunny or rainy when he played around the backyard?
   它在后院玩的时候是晴天还是雨天？

4) Where did he usually play? 它经常在哪里玩？

5) Which part of the body can you call "tummy"?
   你可以叫身体的哪部分为"tummy"？

Look at the picture and mark "O" if it is true and "X" if it is not true.

看图并回答下面的问题，对的打"O"，错的打"X"。

1. On calender it reads "DEC". (   )

2. Total numbers under the calender are "16". (   )

3. Isn't it white color for the shirt of big man on the mural? (   )

4. Is a girl holding a ball on? (   )

5. Two students play music in the studio! (   )

**There are two different pictures left and right on the mural.
But there are many different scenes between them.
You can compare those pictures and give answers below.**

Put the right word in the □. 在空白处填写单词。

1.People are eitheir E□□□□□□□ or G□□□ upstairs.

2. M□□ in the calender downstairs is hung on the wall.

3. What's the color of the flower a man holding on the mural?

   P□□□□□

4. What about the color of his tie?   R□□

5. How many kids are playing games together on the playground?

Completing sentences 完成句子

Match each naming part with an action part to make a sentence.
将每一个名词和行为动词搭配，构成一个句子。

Naming Part	**Action Part**
1. A turtle	sits down.
2. A man	holds a x-ray.
3. A man with the hat	runs very fast.
4. A blanket	is laying on the ground.

Answer Key

Consonants "v, x"
辅音字母 "v, x"

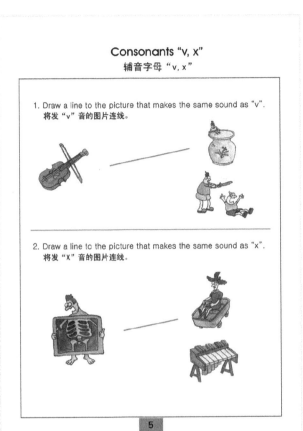

1. Draw a line to the picture that makes the same sound as "v".
   将发 "v" 音的图片连线。

2. Draw a line to the picture that makes the same sound as "x".
   将发 "x" 音的图片连线。

5

Consonants "th, cl"
辅音字母组合 "th, cl"

1. Draw a line to the picture that makes the same sound as "th".
   将发 "th" 音的图片连线。

2. Draw a line to the picture that makes the same sound as "cl".
   将发 "cl" 音的图片连线。

6

Compound Words 复合词

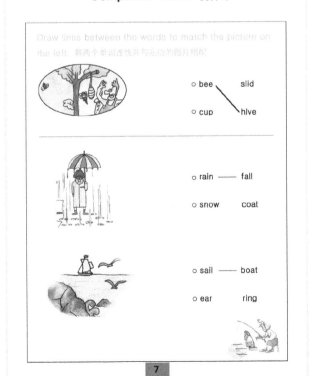

Draw lines between the words to match the picture on the left. 将两个单词连线并与左边的图片相配

o bee   slid

o cup   hive

o rain —— fall

o snow   coat

o sail —— boat

o ear   ring

7

Mixed-up Sentences
顺序混乱的句子

Example

The words in a sentence should be in order.

The bridge, the, over, is, water.

The bridge is over the water.

The words for each sentence are out of order. Write each sentence with words in order.
下列每个句子的单词顺序不对，请按顺序连成一句。

1. swimming, is, A fish
   A fish is swimming.

2. are, trees, two, There
   There are two trees.

8

103

Answer Key

Maze ; Finding alphabet A to Z

Look at the picture below. Help Kenny find alphabet A to Z and also find number 1 to 10 in this picture. All the letters and numbers are hidden under the rocks and trees.

9

找字母 A 到 Z

看图，帮助男孩找到字母 A 到 Z，数字一到十并画圈。

10

Selecting word ending "d"
选择以 "d" 结尾的单词

Take a look at each picture in the box. Circle the same ending sound of the picture above. 看方格里的每一幅图片，将与上面图片相同尾音的图片画圈。

cold

Rhymes: ending"d"

11

Matching word with picture
搭配单词与图片

Name each picture on the left. Read each word on the right. Fill in the circle next to the word with picture. 给左边的每一幅图片命名，读右边的每一个单词，将正确的图片单词前的圆圈涂满。

1.
○ mud
● braid
○ mad

2.
○ shed
○ cod
● rod

3.
○ sad
○ head
● bird

4.
● mad
○ toad
○ cot

5.
○ sad
● bed
○ bird

6.
○ sad
○ head
● toad

Rhymes: ending"d"

12

104

Answer Key

Word recognition-ending "d"
单词辨认 - 以 "d" 结尾的

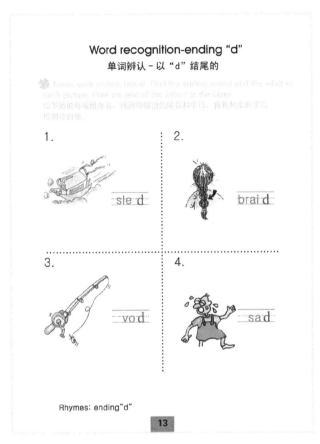

1. sle d
2. brai d
3. ro d
4. sad

Rhymes: ending"d"

13

Making a sentence 造句

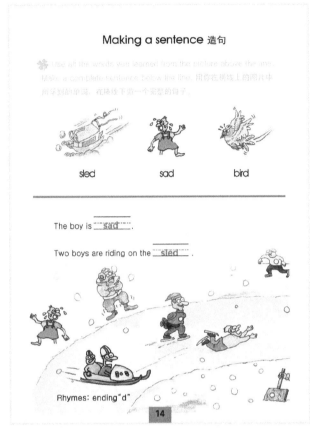

sled   sad   bird

The boy is sad.

Two boys are riding on the sled.

Rhymes: ending"d"

14

Selecting word ending "p"
选择以 "P" 结尾的单词

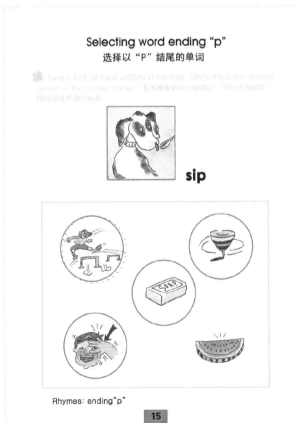

sip

Rhymes: ending"p"

15

Matching word with picture
搭配单词与图片

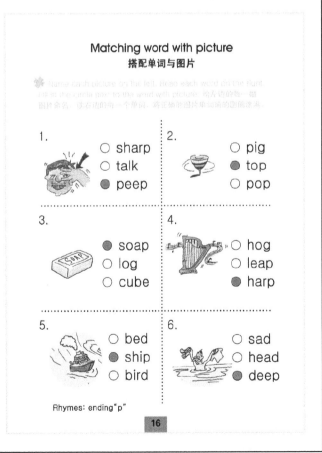

1. ○ sharp ○ talk ● peep
2. ○ pig ● top ○ pop
3. ● soap ○ log ○ cube
4. ○ hog ○ leap ● harp
5. ○ bed ● ship ○ bird
6. ○ sad ○ head ● deep

Rhymes: ending"p"

16

105

Answer Key

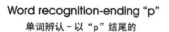

Word recognition-ending "p"
单词辨认 – 以 "p" 结尾的

Name each picture below. Find the ending sound and the letter of each picture. Print the rest of the letters in the blank.
给下面的每幅图命名，找到每幅图的尾音和字母，将其剩余的字母填到空白处。

1. sl_p_

2.  _harp_

3.  _jum_p_

4. _pee_p_

Rhymes: ending "p"

17

Making a sentence 造句

Use all the words you learned from the picture above the line. Make a complete sentence below the line. 用你在横线上的图片中所学到的单词，在横线下造一个完整的句子。

 chimp   peep   harp

A boy is peeping that _chimp_ is playing the _harp_.

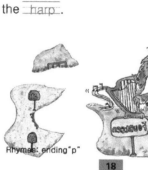

Rhymes: ending "p"

18

Selecting word ending "n"
选择以 "n" 结尾的单词

Take a look at each picture in the box. Circle the same ending sound of the picture above. 看方格里的每一幅图片，将与上面图片相同尾音的图片画圈。

 yarn

Rhymes: ending "n"

19

Matching word with picture
搭配单词与图片

Name each picture on the left. Read each word on the right. Fill in the circle next to the word with picture. 给左边的每一幅图片命名，读右边的每一个单词，将正确的图片单词前的圆圈涂满。

1. ● horn
   ○ phone
   ○ pan

2. ○ bean
   ○ apple
   ● wagon

3. ○ pen
   ● pan
   ○ tan

4. ● raccoon
   ○ clay
   ○ pen

5. ● man
   ○ bed
   ○ bird

6. ○ sad
   ● hen
   ○ toad

Rhymes: ending "n"

20

106

Word recognition-ending "n"
单词辨认 – 以 "n" 结尾的

Name each picture below. Find the ending sound and the letter of each picture. Write the rest of the letters in the blank. 将下面的每幅图命名。找到每幅图的发音和字母，将其余的字母填到空白处。

1.
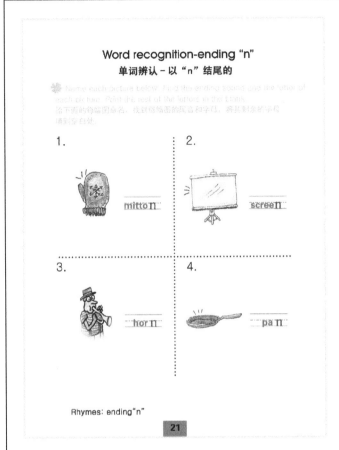
mitto**n**

2.
scree**n**

3.
hor**n**

4.
pa**n**

Rhymes: ending "n"

`21`

Making a sentence 造句

Use all the words you learned from the picture above the line. Make a complete sentence below the line. 用你在横线上的图片中所学到的单词，在横线下造一个完整的句子。

raccoon   horn   wagon

A raccoon blows the horn

on the wagon .

Rhymes: ending "n"

`22`

You can find fun stories below the picture. You can also describe what ever you like.

`23`

Let's have a fun!

`24`

Special Noun and Pronoun
特殊的名词和代词

❀ Naming words include places, persons, animals or things. Look at the word box and fill the word in the blank next to the picture.
给下列单词命名，包括地点、人、动物和事情。看词盒里的单词，在图片旁边的空白处填空。

| kid   school   lock   ox |

Place — school

Person — kid

Thing — lock

Animal — ox

❀ See the pictures and write the words under the line.
看图片在横线下写单词。

A _kid_ is riding on the _ox_ .

`25`

Making a sentence 造句

Read pictures and words above the red line. Make a complete sentence that describe the picture.
读横线上面的单词，造一个完整的句子描述这个图片。

cow   rainbow   window

The _cow_ can see a _rainbow_ after raining.

`26`

Words that describe 描述词

See the picture on the right and describe the scene as much as possible. Fill in the blank with the action verb in the box.
看右边的图，并尽可能多的描述场景。 指出词盒中的行为动词填空。

● She is _carrying_ a turkey.

● The boy is wating to ___pay___ .

● The man is _crying_ .

● The market _displays_ various kinds of vegitables.

● The man who wears suit is _holding_ a paper bag on the top of his head.

| crying, pay, holding carrying, displays |

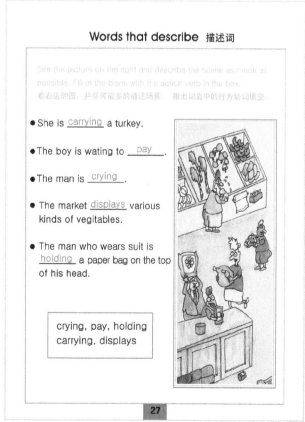

`27`

Naming part / action part
名词 / 动词

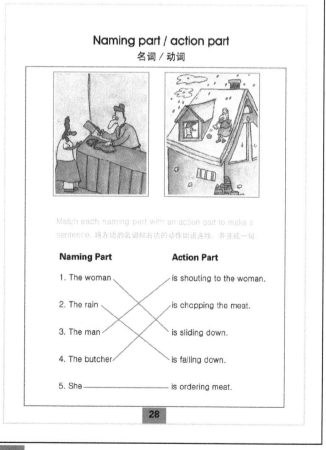

Match each naming part with an action part to make a sentence. 将左边的名词和右边的动作词语连线，并连成一句。

Naming Part	**Action Part**
1. The woman	is shouting to the woman.
2. The rain	is chopping the meat.
3. The man	is sliding down.
4. The butcher	is falling down.
5. She	is ordering meat.

`28`

`108`

Answer Key

Making a sentence 造句

Look at the picture and words above the line. Fill in the blank and make a proper sentence below the line.
看横线上面的图片和单词，在横线下的空白处写下正确的句子。

A boy   strings   ballons

A boy is holding balloons .

29

Making a sentence 造句

Look at the picture and words above the line. Fill in the blank and make a proper sentence below line. 看横线上面的图片和单词，在横线下的空白处写下正确的句子。

Jane   leash   a   dog   walks

She walks a dog .

30

It's ranch 农场

Some children here does what most of kids do in the city. Circle things that does not usually in the ranch. 农场的孩子们和大部分城市的孩子们做的事情一样。将下面不属于农场的事情画圈。

Choose the pictures you have found and then trace and write the words down in the space. 选择你已经找到的图片将单词写到空白处。

golf   tennis   volleyball   hockey

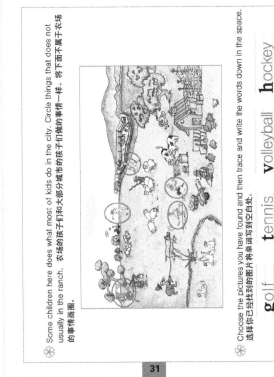

31

Look at the picture below and make your own stories. Compare yours with ours.

Please find me and point to the scene in this picture. I turn into a general holding swords and guns among these little rascals: kicking the ball, targeting the face of the pirate, running over and screwing up somebody's picnic, throwing the ball to the hitter and all the stuffs are messed up... ext.

在图中，你喜欢什么活动？用英语描述！

32

109

Answer Key

Consonants "wh, cr"
辅音字母组合 "wh, cr"

1. Draw a line to the picture that makes the same sound as "wh".
将发 "wh" 音的图片连线。

2. Draw a line to the picture that makes the same sound as "cr".
将发 "cr" 音的图片连线。

35

Finding words from the picture
从图片中找单词

See the picture and find the words from the word box. Write down the words in the blank. 看图从词盒里找出单词，并写到空白处。

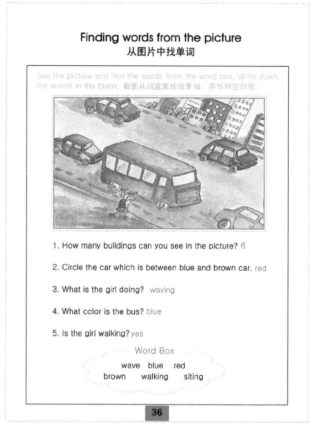

1. How many buildings can you see in the picture? 6

2. Circle the car which is between blue and brown car. red

3. What is the girl doing? waving

4. What color is the bus? blue

5. Is the girl walking? yes

Word Box

wave   blue   red
brown   walking   siting

36

Thinking patterns with the picture
用图片造句

IV. Circle the picture that goes together with the first picture in each row. 将每一行中与第一幅图片可以连成一句的图片画圈。

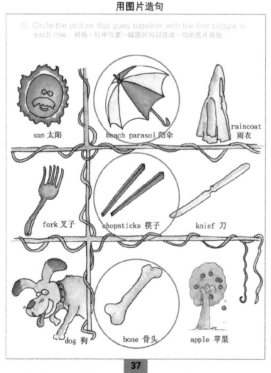

37

Selecting words from the picture
从图片里选单词

Say the name of each picture and choose the right words from word box. Fill in the blank to complete the word. 说出每幅图片的名称，从词盒里选出正确的单词，填空完成单词。

Word box

teacher, poem, hand, point, student

38

110

Answer Key

Finding words from the picture
从图片中找出单词

39

Matching words to the picture
搭配单词与图片

40

Words with picture　图片单词

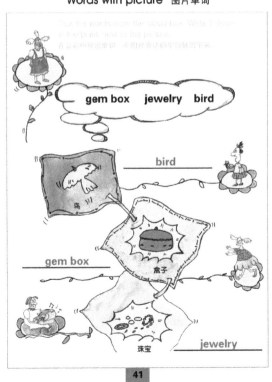

41

Choosing words from the picture
从图片里选择单词

See each picture below and find the proper word next to it.
Circle the word that names each picture and print the word.
看下列每一幅图片，找出其旁边正确的单词，将每幅图片的正确单词画圈，
并写出这个单词。

42

Answer Key

Easy words with picture
简易的单词与图片

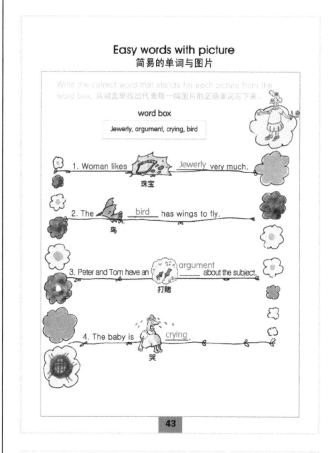

Write the correct word that stands for each picture from the word box. 从词盒里找出代表每一幅图片的正确单词写下来。

word box

Jewerly, argument, crying, bird

1. Woman likes _Jewerly_ very much.
珠宝

2. The _bird_ has wings to fly.
鸟

3. Peter and Tom have an _argument_ about the subject.
打赌

4. The baby is _crying_.
哭

43

It's a farmland! 农场

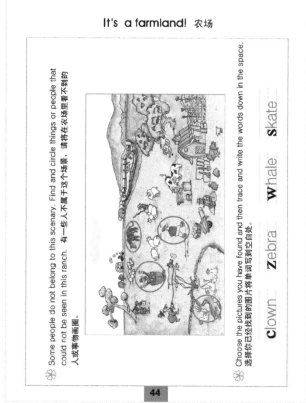

Some people do not belong to this scenary. Find and circle things or people that could not be seen in this ranch. 有一些人不属于这个场景。请将在农场里看不到的人或事物画圈。

Choose the pictures you have found and then trace and write the words down in the space. 选择你已经找到的图片将图片中的单词写到空白处。

clown　zebra　whale　skate

44

Addition and subtraction
加法和减法

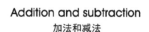

Follow the arrows to count numbers. 跟随箭头数一数

1. How many sharks can you watch?
   If fisherman catches 2 sharks, how many sharks are left?

   _3_

2. How many fishes can you count in all?

   _5_

3. A man in the swimming wants to take 5 fishes out of water.
   How many fishes will be left?

   _0_

45

Naming Words 给单词命名

Look at the picture and fill out the words and then circle the right words. 看图，找出单词并且将正确的单词画圈

1. I do like to _eat_ the food.

(eat)

buy

2. Do you want to go to _top_ of the mountain?

(top)

river

3. I don't _feel_ good.

(feel)

tell

4. I'd like to _read_ the books on the selve.

sell

(read)

46

112

Answer Key

Word game puzzle
字谜游戏

Can you help me solve the crossword puzzle?
你能帮我解开这个字谜游戏吗?

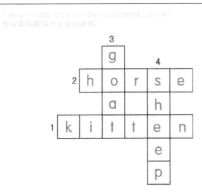

Cross
1. We call cat to this way some times. __kitten__
2. People enjoy riding __horse__ .

Down
3. The animal has two horn. __goat__
4. Sleep is rhyming with __sheep__ .

kitten horse sheep goat

47

Naming part / action part
名词 / 动词

Match each naming part with an action part to make a sentence. 将左边的名词和右边的动作词连线，并造成一句。

Naming Part	Action Part
1. The sign	is making a face.
2. The boy	is standing
3. He	says "Keep off flowers!" .
4. He	is streaching his arms.
5. He	tiptoes cross the garden.

48

Mixed-up Sentences
顺序混乱的句子

Example

The words in a sentence should be in order.

The picture, the, on, hangs, wall.

The picture hangs on the wall.

The words for each sentence are out of order. Write each sentence with correct order. 下列的句子顺序都被调乱了。请改写成一句。

1. The pet, the bed, sits, on.

   The pet sits on the bed.

2. shining, The moon, is.

   The moon is shining.

49

Action verb / Describing pictures
动词 / 描述图片

See the picture above and describe the scene as much as possible. Fill in the blank with the word in the box.
看上面的图片尽量用所描述情景。用下面的话和行为动词填空。

- A man is __donating__ the purse to the begger.

- A dog is __looking__ up the man.

- The begger is __surprised__ at the purse.

- The breard man __thumbs__ up.

- The kid __stops__ riding the skateboard.

thumbs	donating	stops	surprised	looking
冲击	捐赠	停止	惊奇	注视

50

113

Answer Key

Sentence 句子

Look at the picture and circle the right sentence.
看图片，将正确的句子画圈。

1. **(A boy flies high with the swing.)**
   a boy flies high with the swing.

2. **(A boy with red shirt puts a sausage into his uncle Joe's mouth.)**
   a boy with red shirt puts a sausage into his uncle Joe's mouth.

3. a man's hat flies off from his head.
   (A man's hat flies off from his head.)

See the picture above and write the correct words that begins with each the sentence. Write the correct ending mark. 看上面的图片，写出正确的单词开始每个句子，并在结尾写上正确的标点符号。

1. | Who / What | **Who** is eating the sausage **?** |

2. | When / Where | **Where** does the boy play **?** |

`55`

Past tense "ed" and special form of verb
动词的过去式 "ed" 形式和特殊形式

Past tense verbs end in "ed". Look at the picture and underline the verb of past tense and write the past tense verb. 动词的过去式以 "ed" 结尾，看图片将过去式的动词画线，并抄写过去式的动词。

1. We went to the movie.
   went

2. She talked to the man.
   talked

3. He paid the money.
   paid

4. He painted the tree.
   painted

`56`

Using "is" or "are" "is" 或 "are"

See the picture, and fill in the blank using "is" or "are".
看图，并 "is" 和 "are" 填空。

1. There (**is**) a ship sailing on the sea.
2. There (**are**) two animals and one umbrella shown in the picture.
3. The man and the woman (**are**) talking each other.
4. The seal (**is**) spinning the ball on the nose.
5. The chick (**is**) holding the umbrella.
6. The man in the window (**is**) showing his finger and talking to somebody.

`57`

Compound Word 复合词

See the picture in each row. Fill in the line with a correct word to the picture. Make a complete compound word to the line. 看每一行的图片，将图片的正确单词写到横线上组成一个完型的复合词。

cup + cake = **cupcake**

bee + hive = **beehive**

rain + coat = **raincoat**

mail + box = **mailbox**

`58`

Answer Key

Finding words 找单词

See the pictures and the arrows. Move the number of spaces on the arrows. Write the letters to make the complete words.
看下列各子母的箭头和数字，在开始处开始找一个单词。
按箭头上的移动数字代表的位置，并将选出的字母写下来构成完成的单词

sea hay hit eye pay dad

Start

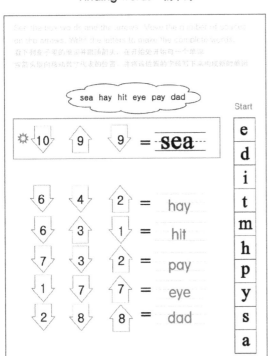

⊛ ↓10 ↑9 ↓9 = **sea**

e
d
i
t
m
h
p
y
s
a

↓6 ↙4 ↑2 = hay
↓6 ↙3 ↑1 = hit
↓7 ↙3 ↑2 = pay
↓1 ↙7 ↑7 = eye
↓2 ↙8 ↑8 = dad

`59`

Word meaning 单词的含义

Choose the word from the word box, and fill the word in the blank. 用词盒里选出的单词，并填到空白处。

jewelry   true   bet   carefully

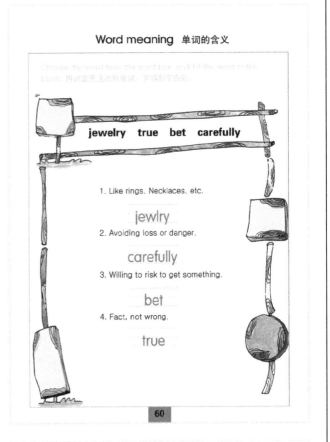

1. Like rings. Necklaces, etc.

jewlry

2. Avoiding loss or danger.

carefully

3. Willing to risk to get something.

bet

4. Fact, not wrong.

true

`60`

Questions/Sentences 问题 / 句子

⊛ Can the sentence be ... Find the correct sentence out on below of 读下列的句子，并找出正确的句子。看图下句线

I)
1. She cradles her baby.
   She cradles her baby?
2. Is she smiling to the baby?
   she is smiling to the baby.
3. There are a pillow in the bed.
   Is there a pillow in the bed?

II)
1. The girls is fatty.
   Is the girl is fatty?
2. The angel play a harp.
   Does she look angry?
3. she is angry.
   Is she angry?

⊛ When the letter begins with the same ... the first letter is capital. Circle the correct letter, and write it on the blank. 每一个单词字下 如果真的时候标识，字可能是大写，将大写的字在后线写在线下面

she / She   She opens the music box   ?
The / the   The kid sits on the roof   .

`63`

Problem solving 解题

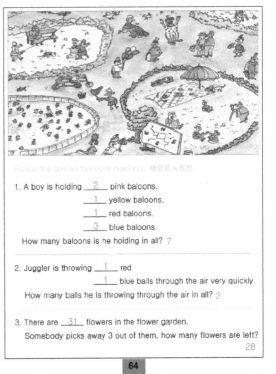

Follow the arrows to count numbers. 根据箭头数数.

1. A boy is holding __2__ pink baloons.
   __1__ yellow baloons.
   __1__ red baloons.
   __3__ blue baloons.
   How many baloons is he holding in all? 7

2. Juggler is throwing __1__ red
   __1__ blue balls through the air very quickly.
   How many balls he is throwing through the air in all? 2

3. There are __31__ flowers in the flower garden.
   Somebody picks away 3 out of them, how many flowers are left?

`28`

`64`

116

Answer Key

Addition 加法

Find the missing number that makes the number sentence true and fill in the bubble with the right answer. 选择所缺数字使下列格式正确, 并将正确答案前的圆圈涂满.

1.
2 + 5 = ☐
2 7 9 11
○ ● ○ ○

2.
3 + 7 = ☐
2 7 9 10
○ ○ ○ ●

Add the number and use counters if you like. 加数字.

4 + 9 = 13
3 + 3 = 6
4 + 4 = 8
7 + 2 = 9

0 + 7 = 7
3 + 8 = 8
3 + 5 = 8
5 + 3 = 8

See the picture below and solve the problem. 看下列图片解题.

 5

1. There are 7 birds and 3 sheep. How many animals are there in all?
10

2. There are 3 bees and 3 sheep. How many bees and sheep in all?
6

69

Sentence 句子

Look at this picture. Draw a line under each question sentence and then answer the following questions. 看这幅图片, 在每一个问题下划线并回答下列问题.

1. What does the kid play?
The drum
2. What does he hold?
drumsticks
3. He is sad.

Look at this picture. Draw a line under each question and answer the following questions. 看这幅图片, 在每一个问题下划线并回答下列问题.

1. Is she brave or scarry?
scarry
2. Why she is so scarry?
Because there is a snake.

Cumulative review/Question

70

Descriptive 描述

Look at the pictures below. Write the right adjective that describes each picture and write down the words on the line. 看下列图片写出描述每幅图片的正确的形容词并写在线线上.

cute	scared	smile	danger
可爱的	害怕的	微笑	危险

1. It is (danger) for him to play in the middle of the road.
2. The driver is so (scared) of the boy jumping into the car.
3. Mom is giving her (smile) to her baby.
4. The baby is so (cute).

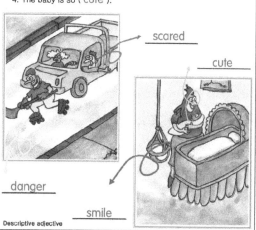

scared
cute
danger
smile

Descriptive adjective

71

Word game puzzle 字谜游戏

Find the name of each picture in the puzzle box. You can also use the reference words related to each puzzle word. The word may go across or down. In the puzzle box. 在字谜盒中找出每幅图片的名字, 你可以使用与每一个字谜单词相关的参考单词, 每个单词在字谜盒中横竖列都可以.

w	e	b		f	a	n
		u		o		e
	s	o	x			s
						t

Reference Box

spider	car	cool
smart	feet	bird

72

118

Answer Key

Adjective 形容词

Look at the pictures below. Write the adjective that describes each picture and write down the words on the line.
看一看的图片。写出描绘每幅图片的形容词并写在线上。

sleepy	high	tasty	bald	slippery	fatty
困的	高的	美味的	光头的	滑的	肥胖的

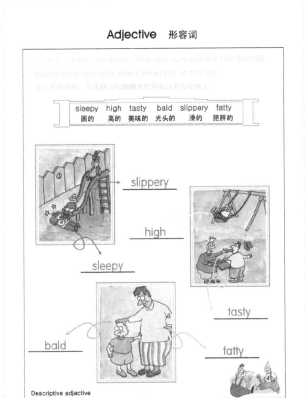

slippery

high

sleepy

tasty

bald

fatty

Descriptive adjective

73

Naming part / action part
名词 / 动词

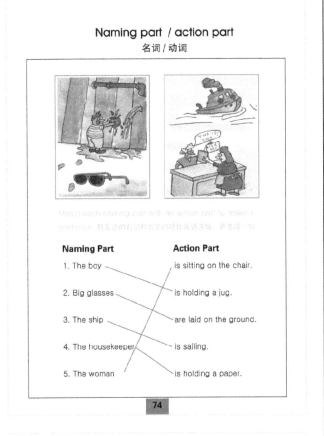

Match each naming part with an action part to make a sentence. 将左边的名词和右边的动词连接连线，并连成一句。

Naming Part	Action Part
1. The boy	is sitting on the chair.
2. Big glasses	is holding a jug.
3. The ship	are laid on the ground.
4. The housekeeper	is sailing.
5. The woman	is holding a paper.

74

Completing sentences
完成句子

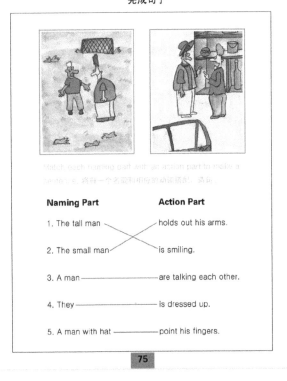

Match each naming part with an action part to make a sentence. 将每一个名词和相应动词连接，连成。

Naming Part	Action Part
1. The tall man	holds out his arms.
2. The small man	is smiling.
3. A man	are talking each other.
4. They	Is dressed up.
5. A man with hat	point his fingers.

75

Consonants "sn, sp"
辅音字母组合 "sn, sp"

1. Draw a line to the picture that makes the same sound as "sn".
将与 "sn" 发音相同的图片连线。

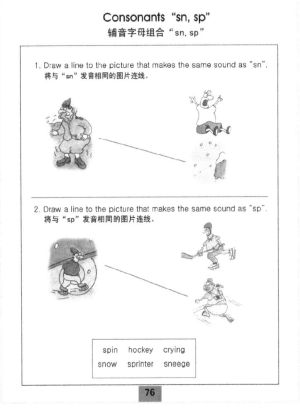

2. Draw a line to the picture that makes the same sound as "sp".
将与 "sp" 发音相同的图片连线。

spin	hockey	crying
snow	sprinter	sneege

76

119

Answer Key

Let's do shopping 让我们购物吧！

People are shopping in the market. Some items are not sold in this store. Circle the items which do not belong to the supermarket. 人们正在商场购物。有一些商品在这家商场没有把不属于这家超市的商品画圈。

Choose the pictures you have found, trace and write the words down in the space. 选择你已经找到的图片将单词写到空白处。

Sheep Chicken rabbit sack radish

77

Vowel sound "i" 长元音"i"

"kite" has long a "i" sound. Name each picture and circle the picture which has the long "i" sound. Choose the word from the word box and write it in on the line next to the picture.
"kite"含有长元音"i"; 给每幅图片命名，将含有长元音 "i"的图片画圈。

Biting is fun.

word box

time,cry,busy,find,fly,smile

时间 time

笑 smile

飞 fly

哭 cry

找 find

忙 busy

78

Finding acting verbs 找出行为动词

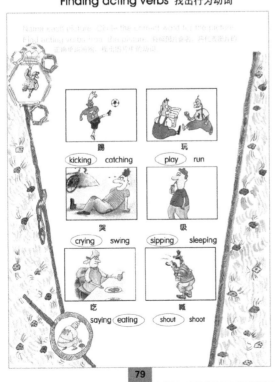

Name each picture. Circle the correct word for the picture. Find acting verbs in this picture. 给每幅图片命名，圈出正确的单词。找出图片中的动词。

踢 kicking catching

玩 play run

哭 crying swing

吸 sipping sleeping

吃 saying eating

喊 shout shoot

79

Descriptive verbs from the picture
描述图片的动词

Circle the action verb which resemble the motion from the word box. Write it on the line. 从词组中找出描述行为的动词，将其写下单词。

word box

sweating, running, sleeping, sitting, exercising, delivering.

运动 exercising

跑 running

睡 sleeping

流汗 sweating

送 delivering

坐 sitting

80

Answer Key

81

Vowel 元音音韵

Read the sentence and see whether the underlined word is spelled right or wrong. Write the correct word on the line if it is wrong.
读句子，看一下化线单词的拼写是否是正确的单词。

Left o→right, right ●→wrong

1. There is a big <u>hiv</u> on the tree

   hive

2. It's a <u>sunny</u> day.

   sunny

3. The mom bear is <u>shaking</u> a tree.

   shaking

4. Three bees are <u>buzing</u> all around.

   buzzing

5. A baby bear can't wait to eat <u>hony</u>.

   honey

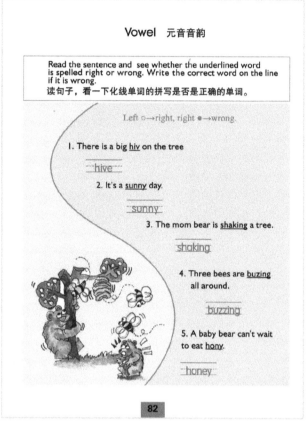

82

Selecting words with picture
选择正确的图片单词

See the picture and find the word in the word box.
看图并在词盒中找出单词。

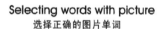

1. How many buildings can you see in the picture? (6)

2. Circle the car which is between blue bus and brown car.

3. What is she doing ? She is waving.

4. What color is the bus ? blue

5. Is she walking or sitting?

   She is sitting.

   Waving, blue, red, brown, walking, siting.

83

Ending consonant review
复习辅音结尾的单词

Take a look at each picture. Choose and circle the right ending consonant to the picture.

看每一幅图片，选择图片名称的正确辅音尾音，并画圈。

84

Vowel A (ai/ay)
元音 A(ai/ay)

Read the sentence in each row with the picture; circle and write the word in the sentence.

读句子，将符合句意的正确单词画圈，并写在句子中。

- play
- grey
- cry

1. Boys ( ) the table tennis.

2. Train runs the ( ) road.

- rail
- tray
- sail

3. When do you ( ) your boat?

- pail
- snail
- sail

4. He ( ) the bill at the counter.

- plain
- pay
- play

5. A ( ) will fly to the sky.

- trail
- pail
- quail

85

Long a (ay and ai)
长元音 a（ay and ai）

Say the name of the picture above the line.

说出横线上图片的名称。

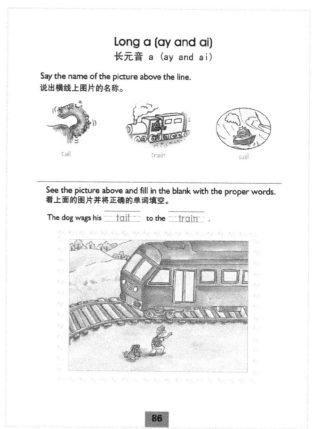

tail   train   sail

See the picture above and fill in the blank with the proper words.

看上面的图片并将正确的单词填空。

The dog wags his ___tail___ to the ___train___ .

86

89

90

Finding words 找单词

Read the box words to follow the arrows. Begin each word at Start. Move the number of spaces on the arrows and write the letters to make words. 看下列盒子里的单词并跟随箭头。在开始处开始每一个单词，按数字指向移动数字代表的位置，并将该位置的字母写下来构成新的单词。

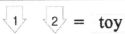

☼ 2↓ 1↓ 2↓ = **toy**

Start

e
t
o
r
y
n
h
a
b
c

10↓ 2↑ 6↑ = cat
6↓ 5↑ 1↓ = net
3↓ 5↑ 6↑ = oat
10↓ 2↑ 1↑ = cab
7↓ 4↑ 1↑ = hot

91

Finding words 找单词

Read the box words to follow the arrows. Begin each word at Start. Move the number of spaces on the arrows and write the letters to make words. 看下列盒子里的单词并跟随箭头。在开始处开始每一个单词，按数字指向移动数字代表的位置，并将该位置的字母写下来构成新的单词。

pay day tea say dad sat

Start

e
i
t
r
u
y
s
a
p
d

☼ 9↓ 1↑ 2↑ = **pay**

10↓ 2↑ 2↑ = day
3↓ ↑ 7↓ = tea
7↓ 1↑ 2↓ = say
10↓ 2↑ 2↑ = dad
7↓ 1↑ 5↑ = sat

92

Finding words 找单词

Read the words box to follow the arrows. Begin each word at start. Move the number of spaces on the arrows and write the letters to make words. 读下列盒子里的单词并跟随箭头。请在结尾开始的一个单词，按数字指向移动数字代表的位置，并将该位置的字母写下来构成新的单词。

may did key sit pit kit

start

e
d
i
t
m
k
p
y
s
a

☼ 5↓ 5↓ 2↑ = **may**

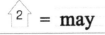

2↓ 1↓ 1↓ = did
6↓ 5↑ 7↓ = key
9↓ 6↑ 1↓ = sit
7↓ 4↑ 1↓ = pit
6↓ 3↑ 1↓ = kit

93

Questions and subtraction 减法题

※ Question 1 问题 1
9 pigs are eating food around the pen. If pigs eat all, 3 set out from the pen after they finished their dinner. how many pigs are still eating now? 有两只小猪正在花园里吃着东西，有两只小猪在它们吃完后离开了，现在有几只小猪还在吃东西？ 我在这剩几只小猪还在吃东西：

There are two pigs.

※ Question 2 问题 2
There are 6 cats in the living room. Sam, sister took 3 cats out. How many cats are left there? 客厅里有6只猫，Sam的妹妹拿走了3只猫。现在还剩几只？

There are three.

※ Question 3 问题 3
Find the missing number that makes the number sentence true, and fill the bubble in the right answer. 找出缺少的数字，使列式正确，将它填在要涂的地方涂满。

1.   8 − [5] = 3
5   2   1   4
●   ○   ○   ○

2.   9 − [6] = 3
3   4   6   7
○   ○   ●   ○

94

Answer Key

Addition 加法

❋Question1) 问题1
There are 7 birds in the trees. 2 more birds just flew down to sit on the same branch. How many birds are there in total？
树上有7只鸟，又有2只飞过来坐到了同一个树干上，一共有多少只鸟？

__There are nine birds.__

❋Question 2) 问题2
8 puppies came Tom's door. There were 2 dogs there sipping the soup. How many dogs are there in total?
8只小狗来到了汤姆家的门口，在那儿有2只狗在喝汤，一共有几只狗？

__There are ten.__

❋Question 3) 问题3
Find the missing number that makes the number sentence true and fill the bubble in the right answer. 找出缺少的数字，使列式正确，将正确的答案前的圆圈涂满。

1.
$$7 + \boxed{2} = 9$$
1　2　3　4
○　●　○　○

2.
$$8 + \boxed{2} = 10$$
4　2　9　11
○　●　○　○

95

Question of the sentence 问题

❋Question1) 问题1
Read the sentence. Write the word that matches each meaning from the word box. 用词盒里的单词，完成下列句子

| eagerly, slowly, loudly, peeping, lonely, seen. |

1. You must drive your car __slowly__ when you see the school bus.

2. The doggy inside of the box is __peeping__ out.

❋Question 2) 问题2
Use the word from the word box above and print it with the same meaning.

1. Feel sad __lonely__ .

2. Very interested in doing something __seen__ .

96

suffixes 后缀

❋Question1) 问题1
Suffixes are added to the end of a word to change its meaning: "ful, ly." 在词后面加后缀，可以改变词的意思。

1. A dog is __licking__ a bone __eagerly__ .

2. Sometime, she feels __lonely__ .

3. The dog __chased__ a cat __quickly__ .

4. The man __carry__ the dog __carefully__ .

| licking, carefully, quickly, carry, eagerly, chased, lonely. |

97

A dog taken to the vet 小狗去看兽医

One slightly wet and moist day, the dog, Kenny caught a terrible cold. He was so wet when he splashed into the puddle at the backyard the other day. Since it rained heavily all over the place where he usually played well. He sneezed hard and had a fever. So he was brought to the vet. He was taken not once, not even twice, but more than 5 times. He had a spoonful of medicine not once, he had six spoonful of medicine.

Sara, the kenny's owner worried about him. She rolled him back and force to check out his body. She caressed and strocked his back gently and lovingly. She patted his tummy several times saying "poor little puppy".

98

124

Answer Key

A dog taken to the vet 小狗去看兽医

1) How much medicine did Kenny take? 它吃了多少药?
   six
2) Why did he go to the vet? 它为什么要去看兽医?
   She had a trebble cold.
3) Was it sunny or rainy when he played around the backyard?
   它在后院玩的时候是晴天还是雨天?
   rainy
4) Where did he usually play? 它经常在哪里玩?
   in the backyard.
5) Which part of body can you call "tummy"?
   你可以叫身体的哪部分为 "tummy"?
   stomach

99

Look at the picture and mark "O"; fit's true and "X" if it's not true.
看图并回答下面的问题，对的打 "O"，错的打 "X"。

1. On calender it reads "DEC". (O)
. The number calender it says "16". (X)
3. Isn't it write color for the shirt of big man on the mural? (O)
4. Is girl holding a ball on? (X)
5. Two students play music in the studio! (O)

100

Drawing in English

There are two different pictures left and right on the mural.
But there are many different scenes between them.
You can compare those pictures and give answers below.

Put the right word in the □. 在空白处填写单词。

1. People are either **Exercize** or **Game** upstairs.
. **May** in the calender downstairs is hung on the wall.
3. What's the color of the flower a man holding on the mural?
   Purple
. What about the color of his tie? **Red**
5. How many kids are playing games together on the playground? 4

101

Completing sentences 完成句子

Match each naming part with an action part to make a sentence.
将每一个名词相门与动词搭配，构成一个句子。

Naming Part	Action Part
1. A turtle	sits down.
2. A man	holds a x-ray.
3. A man with the hat	runs very fast.
4. A blanket	is laying on the ground.

102

Consonants "v, x"
辅音字母 "v, x"

1. Draw a line to the picture that makes the same sound as "v".
将发 "v" 音的图片连线。

2. Draw a line to the picture that makes the same sound as "x".
将发 "x" 音的图片连线。

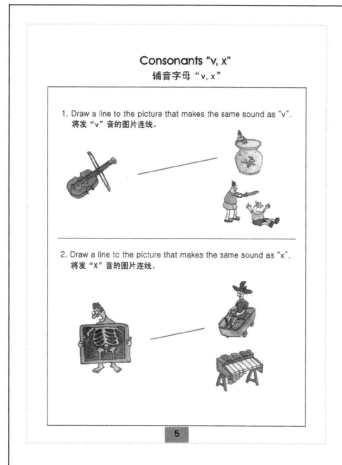

5

Printed in the USA
CPSIA information can be obtained
at www.ICGtesting.com
CBHW060130111024
15668CB00057B/1190